TERRORISM: Origins and Future.

By Boris Romanov

An analysis of the ideology and practices of contemporary terrorism shows the amazing coincidences with the ideology and methods of struggle of the Russian revolutionary of XIX century Sergey Nechayev, who wrote the "Catechism of a Revolutionary" (the book was published in 1871). As for today's terrorists, who fight against the western civilization, as can be seen, "Catechism of a Revolutionary" is fully consistent with the ideology and methods of their struggle. Many of the provisions and recommendations of the "Catechism" literally fit their methods of struggle. We do not know, whether the ideologists and leaders of modern terrorists read this "Catechism", but it is so.

On the other hand, some modern esoteric claim that around the beginning of XXI century began "era of separation" between Good and Evil, which replaced "era of mixing" of Good and Evil, which lasted about 2,160 years (150 BC - 2007\2008 year AD). How long will last the era of separation, and how this relates to the age of the apocalypse foretold in the Book of Revelation of Holy Bible?

The author examines in detail all of these questions in this brochure.

Content

We will not to tell here the history of terrorism from the most ancient times. Let's start this review from a new time.

The periodization of new and modern era of terrorism

Political scientists identify four global wave of modern and contemporary periods of terrorism:

1.   The first wave of terrorism associated with the spread in the 1880s, first in Russia and then in Europe and North America the revolutionary ideologies (sometimes united under the name of anarchism, though neither Russian Populists (Russian revolutionary organizations of those years), nor the Irish revolutionary organizations were not anarchists in the strict sense of the word). In the last chapter ("Russian roots of terrorism"), we will consider in detail the Russian source of modern terrorism, associated primarily with the history of Sergey Nechayev, who was the prototype of the hero of the famous novel "Demons" by Fyodor Dostoevsky.

2.   The second wave of terrorism has been associated with anti-colonial, the national liberation movement of the XX century, and (parallel) with the activities of the Comintern (aka "Third International", 1919-1943 years), which by all means tried to weaken the Western world, including supporting anti-colonialism . Created by Lenin (the main follower of Sergei Nechayev), the Comintern was largely heir anti-bourgeois ideas and methods of struggle of Sergei Nechayev and his "*Catechism of a Revolutionary*".

The Comintern was involved in the revolutions across Europe in this period (especially in 1919-1930 years), starting with the Hungarian Soviet Republic in 1919. Several hundred agitators and financial aid were sent from the Soviet Union and Lenin was in regular contact with its leader, Béla Kun. Soon an official "**Terror**

Group of the Revolutionary Council of the Government" was formed, unofficially known as "Lenin Boys".["The Black Book of Communism," pp. 272-5]

3. The third wave of terrorism has been linked to the activities of the so-called "New Left" in the 1970s. Although the "New Left" had their own ideologists, but their anti-bourgeois ideology and methods of struggle were associated (as the original sources) with the same "Catechism of a Revolutionary". The movement of the "New Left" have had significant impact on the development of the left-radical terrorism of the 1970s ("Red Army Faction" in Germany, "Red Brigades" in Italy, etc.).

4. The fourth wave of terrorism began in the 1990s, as the struggle against globalization and against the "Western values." This wave began and continues as a religious (alleged Islamist) terrorism. However, if we carefully read the "Catechism of a Revolutionary" (by Sergei Nechayev), we'll see that even these modern terrorists are in fact in a sense the heirs of the "Catechism of a Revolutionary"

***

On the other hand, the new and modern history of terrorism is associated with the transition of all mankind from the "Era of mixing" to the "Era of separation." This esoteric concept of the history of mankind is also very important for the understanding of contemporary terrorism, and we'll consider this concept below.

But at first we'll tell about Sergey Nechayev's history and his "Revolutionary Catechism". This is all the more important that just Nechayev was the prototype of the main character of "Demons" by Dostoevsky.

Russian roots of terrorism

(Machiavelli – Nechayev – Lenin – Stalin – and others later.)[1]

"Politics and morality are incompatible", *"Politics is a dirty*

---

1   Earlier this part of this brochure was published (by me) under the title "History of immorality in politics"

business ... it has always been and so it will" – such opinions are very often you can hear from a variety of people. More educated people can add that it was at least from the time of Machiavelli. However, in the early XX century, the word "Machiavellianism" was considered a dirty word synonymous with immorality in politics. But immorality (in Russian) is only indifferent to morality, it is not synonymous of amorality, not synonymous with dirty and amoral policy. When and who made politics as a dirty business?

The author believes that the theoretical and practical bases of amorality in the policy were laid down in the 1870s by Russian revolutionary Sergey Nechayev (prototype of the protagonist in the novel "Demons" by Dostoevsky). Then Vladimir Lenin after 1917 fully embodied the "revolutionary catechism" (by Nechayev) in life and in real politics. Later amoral principles also captured global policies too. It is still going on.

Of course, and before Machiavelli (earlier the XV century) "powers" (power rulers of the world) in their policy were not always guided by moral principles – but before Machiavelli's time an immorality in politics was not publicly proclaimed as the norm (as required principle in the policy and as the "true" reality real policy).

Whether the policy was always amoral?

Machiavelli and machiavellianism.

Niccolo di Bernardo dei Machiavelli (1469 – 1527) was an Italian historian, politician, diplomat, philosopher, humanist, and writer based in Florence during the Renaissance. He was for many years an official in the Florentine Republic, with responsibilities in diplomatic and military affairs. He was a founder of modern political science, and more specifically political ethics. He also wrote comedies, carnival songs, and poetry. His personal correspondence is renowned in the Italian language. He was Secretary to the Second Chancery of the Republic of Florence from 1498 to 1512, when the Medici were out of power. He wrote his masterpiece, The Prince, after the Medici had recovered power and he no longer held a position of responsibility in Florence.

Niccolo di Bernardo dei Machiavell

"Machiavellianism" is a widely used negative term to characterize unscrupulous politicians of the sort Machiavelli described in The Prince. The book itself gained enormous notoriety and wide readership because the author seemed to be endorsing behavior often deemed as evil and immoral.

Machiavellianism is one of the three personality traits referred to as the dark triad, along with narcissism and psychopathy. Some psychologists consider Machiavellianism to be essentially a subclinical form of psychopathy.

Anyway, afier XVI century, the Machiavellianism called the policy based on pragmatism and cynicism, on the cult of power and neglecting moral norms. As we have noted above, up to the beginning of XX century (more precisely - up to 1917), the word "Machiavellianism" in Russia (and the world) has had negative, even among many politicians, not to mention the general population - for the most educated people it was just a dirty word.

Machiavellianism in Russia (till 1917)

Modern Russian cynics (who believe that politics has always been a messy affair for all politicians and for all people) - these cynics forget that Machiavelli's major works were published in Russia only in 1869 - two years before the trial of the revolutionary Sergey Nechayev (prototype of Peter Verkhovenskii of "Demons" Dostoevsky). But even the Russian revolutionaries are mostly not taken Machiavellianism in those years, and Nechayev was accused of immoral following these principles. I will not mention the non-revolutionaries: Russian educated society at the time (post-reform years reign of Emperor Alexander II) perceived the Machiavelli's books as monstrous immorality (which it actually is).

This attitude towards politics and politicians - a policy must be moral! - prevailed in the Russian society almost up to 1917. And only the followers of Sergei Nechayev took him terribly amoral "Catechism of a Revolutionary."

Sergey Nechayev

(Excerpts from the Wikipedia article about Sergei Nechayev, with my comments)

Sergey Nechayev (October 2, 1847 – November 21 or December 3, 1882) was a Russian revolutionary associated with the Nihilist movement and known for his single-minded pursuit of revolution by any means necessary, including political violence.

Nechayev organized the first Russian student demonstrations against the government (in St. Petersburg). He knew and worked with such prominent Russian revolutionaries as Vera Zasulich, and later (in Geneva) with Mikhail Bakunin and Alexander Herzen. Herzen disliked Nechayev's fanaticism and strongly opposed the campaign, believing Nechayev was influencing Bakunin toward more extreme rhetoric.

In late spring 1869, Nechayev wrote Catechism of a Revolutionary, a program for the "merciless destruction" of society and the state. The main principle of the "Catechism"—"***the ends*** *justify the means*"—became Nechayev's slogan throughout his revolutionary career. He believed that the struggle must be carried out by any means necessary, with an unwavering focus on their destruction. The individual self is to be subsumed by a greater purpose in a kind of spiritual asceticism, which for Nechayev was far more than just a theory, but the guiding principle by which he lived his life.

Having left Russia illegally, Nechayev had to sneak back to Moscow via Romania in August 1869 with help from Bakunin's underground contacts.

In Moscow he lived an austere life, spending the fund only on political activities. He pretended to be a proxy of the Russian department of the "Worldwide Revolutionary Union" (which didn't exist) and created an affiliate of a secret society called Narodnaya Rasprava (Народная расправа, "People's Reprisal"), which, he claimed, had existed for quite some time in every corner of Russia. He spoke passionately to student dissidents about the need to organise.

Many were impressed by the young proletarian and joined the group. However, the already fanatical Nechayev appeared to be becoming more distrustful of the people around him, even denouncing Bakunin as doctrinaire, "idly running off at the mouth and on paper". One Narodnaya Rasprava member, I. I. Ivanov, disagreed with Nechayev about the distribution of propaganda, and left the group. On November 21, 1869, Nechayev and several comrades beat, strangled and shot Ivanov, hiding the body in a lake through a hole in the ice. This incident was fictionalised by writer Fyodor Dostoyevsky in his political novel, Demons, published three years later, in which the character, Pyotr Stepanovich Verkhovensky, is based on Nechayev.

The body was soon found, and some of his colleagues arrested, but Nechayev eluded capture, and left for Saint Petersburg in late November where he tried to continue his activities to create a clandestine society. On December 15, 1869, he fled the country, heading back to Geneva.

Nechayev was embraced by Bakunin and Ogarev on his return to Switzerland in January 1870. Soon after their reunion, Herzen died, and a large fund from his personal wealth was made available to Nechayev to continue his political activities. Nechayev issued a number of proclamations aimed at different strata of the Russian population. Together with Ogarev, he published the Kolokol magazine (April–May, 1870, issues 1 to 6). In his article "The Fundamentals of the Future Social System" (Главные основы будущего общественного строя), published in the People's Reprisal (1870, №2), Nechayev shared his vision of a communist system which **Karl Marx and Friedrich Engels would later call "barracks communism"**.

However Nechayev's suspicion of his comrades had grown even greater, and he began stealing letters and private papers with which to blackmail Bakunin and his fellow exiles, should the need arise. He enlisted the help of Herzen's daughter Natalie. While clearly not breaking with Nechayev, Bakunin rebuked Nechayev upon discovery of his duplicity: "Lies, cunning [and] entanglement [are] a necessary and marvelous means for demoralising and destroying the enemy, though certainly not a useful means of obtaining and attracting new friends".

In September 1870, Nechayev published an issue of the Commune magazine in London and later, hiding from the tsarist police, went underground in Paris and then Zurich.

On August 14, 1872, Nechayev was arrested in Zurich and handed over to the Russian police. He was found guilty on January 8, 1873, and sentenced to 20 years of katorga (hard labor) for killing Ivanov. Nechayev, while locked up in a ravelin of the Peter and Paul Fortress, managed to win over his guards with the strength of his convictions, and by the late 1870s, he was using them to pass on correspondence with revolutionaries on the outside. In December 1880, Nechayev established contact with the Executive Committee of Narodnaya Volya and proposed a plan for his escape. However, he abandoned the plan due to his unwillingness to distract the efforts of the members of Narodnaya Volya from attempting to assassinate Alexander II.

In 1882, Nechayev died in his cell.

Despite his personal courage and fanatical dedication to the revolutionary cause, Nechayev's methods (later called Nechayevshchina) were viewed to have caused harm to the Russian revolutionary movement by endangering clandestine organizations.

Nechayev's methods and ideas have been successfully implemented by many revolutionaries including Vladimir Lenin and Joseph Stalin.

Sergey Nechayev

Catechism of a Revolutionary

The manifesto is an authoritarian manual for the formation of secret societies.

Its publication in the Government Herald in July 1871 as the manifesto of the Narodnaya Rasprava secret society was one of the most dramatic events of Nechayev's revolutionary life,[1][2] through its words and the actions it inspired establishing Nechayev's importance for the Nihilist movement. The Catechism is divided into two sections; General Rules of the Organisation and Rules of Conduct of Revolutionaries, 22 and 26 paragraphs long respectively.

The most radical document of its age, the Catechism outlined the authors' revolutionary Jacobin program of organisation and discipline, a program that became the backbone of the radical movement in Russia. The revolutionary is portrayed in the Catechism as an amoral avenging angel, an expendable resource in the service of the revolution, committed to any crime or treachery necessary to effect the downfall of the prevailing order.

Thus, the "Catechism of a Revolutionary," was first published in Geneva in 1869 [3]. Since it began in Russia and scrapped moral core in the political struggle. Let us read excerpts from this "instruction basic truths" revolutionary.

Below I quote Catechism of a Revolutionary" from the text https://www.marxists.org/subject/anarchism/nechayev/catechism.ht m

Below I have highlighted **in bold** those provisions of the "Catechism", which relate entirely in full to modern terrorists who are fighting against Western civilization.

The Duties of the Revolutionary toward Himself

*1. **The revolutionary is a doomed man. He has no personal interests, no business affairs, no emotions, no attachments, no property, and no name. Everything in him is wholly absorbed in the single thought and the single passion for revolution.***

*2.   The revolutionary knows that in the very depths of his being, not only in words but also in deeds, he has broken all the bonds which tie him to the social order and the civilized world with all its laws, moralities, and customs, and with all its generally accepted conventions. **He is their implacable enemy, and if he continues to live with them it is only in order to destroy them more speedily.***

*3.   The revolutionary despises all doctrines and refuses to accept the mundane sciences, leaving them for future generations. **He knows only one science: the science of destruction**. For this reason, but only for this reason, he will study mechanics, physics, chemistry, and perhaps medicine. But all day and all night he studies the vital science of human beings, their characteristics and circumstances, and all the phenomena of the present social order.*

The object is perpetually the same: the surest and quickest way of destroying the whole filthy order.

*4.   The revolutionary despises public opinion. He despises and hates the existing social morality in all its manifestations. **For him, morality is everything which contributes to the triumph of the revolution**. Immoral and criminal is everything that stands in its way.*

5.   The revolutionary is a dedicated man, merciless toward

the State and toward the educated classes; and he can expect no mercy from them. **Between him and them there exists, declared or concealed, a relentless and irreconcilable war to the death. He must accustom himself to torture.**

6. *Tyrannical toward himself,* **he must be tyrannical toward others. All the gentle and enervating sentiments of kinship, love, friendship, gratitude, and even honor, must be suppressed in him and give place to the cold and singleminded passion for revolution. For him, there exists only one pleasure, on consolation, one reward, one satisfaction -- the success of the revolution.** *Night and day he must have but one thought, one aim -- merciless destruction.* **Striving cold-bloodedly and indefatigably toward this end, he must be prepared to destroy himself and to destroy with his own hands everything that stands in the path of the revolution.**

7. *The nature of the true revolutionary excludes all sentimentality, romanticism, infatuation, and exaltation. All private hatred and revenge must also be excluded. Revolutionary passion, practiced at every moment of the day until it becomes a habit, is to be employed with cold calculation.* **At all times, and in all places, the revolutionary must obey not his personal impulses, but only those**

The Relations of the Revolutionary toward his Comrades

8. *The revolutionary can have no friendship or attachment, except for those who have proved by their actions that they, like him, are dedicated to revolution. The degree of friendship, devotion and obligation toward such a comrade is determined solely by the degree of his usefulness to the cause of total revolutioary destruction.*

9. *It is superfluous to speak of solidarity among revolutionaries. The whole strength of revolutionary work lies in this. Comrades who possess the same revolutionary passion and understanding should, as much as possible, deliberate all important matters together and come to unanimous conclusions.* **When the plan is finally decided upon, then the revolutionary must rely solely on himself. In carrying out acts of destruction, each one should act alone, never running to another for advice and assistance,**

except when these are necessary for the furtherance of the plan.

10. All revolutionaries should have under them second- or third-degree revolutionaries -- i.e., comrades who are not completely initiated. these should be regarded as part of the common revolutionary capital placed at his disposal. This capital should, of course, be spent as economically as possible in order to derive from it the greatest possible profit. The real revolutionary should regard himself as capital consecrated to the triumph of the revolution; however, he may not personally and alone dispose of that capital without the unanimous consent of the fully initiated comrades.

11. When a comrade is in danger and the question arises whether he should be saved or not saved, the decision must not be arrived at on the basis of sentiment, but solely in the interests of the revolutionary cause. Therefore, it is necessary to weigh carefully the usefulness of the comrade against the expenditure of revolutionary forces necessary to save him, and the decision must be made accordingly.

The Relations of the Revolutionary toward Society

12. The new member, having given proof of his loyalty not by words but by deeds, can be received into the society only by the unanimous agreement of all the members.

13. The revolutionary enters the world of the State, of the privileged classes, of the so-called civilization, and he lives in this world only for the purpose of bringing about its speedy and total destruction. He is not a revolutionary if he has any sympathy for this world. **He should not hesitate to destroy any position, any place, or any man in this world. He must hate everyone and everything in it with an equal hatred.** *All the worse for him if he has any relations with parents, friends, or lovers; he is no longer a revolutionary if he is swayed by these relationships.*

14. Aiming at implacable revolution, the revolutionary may and frequently must live within society will pretending to be completely different from what he really is, for he must penetrate everywhere, into all the higher and middle-classes, into the houses of commerce, the churches, and the palaces of the aristocracy, and into the worlds of the bureaucracy and literature and the military, and also into the Third Division and the Winter Palace of the Czar.

15. *This filthy social order can be split up into several categories. The first category comprises those who must be condemned to death without delay. Comrades should compile a list of those to be condemned according to the relative gravity of their crimes; and the executions should be carried out according to the prepared order.*

16. *When a list of those who are condemned is made, and the order of execution is prepared, no private sense of outrage should be considered, nor is it necessary to pay attention to the hatred provoked by these people among the comrades or the people.* **Hatred and the sense of outrage may even be useful insofar as they incite the masses to revolt.** *It is necessary to be guided only by the relative usefulness of these executions for the sake of revolution. Above all, those who are especially inimical to the revolutionary organization must be destroyed; their violent and sudden deaths will produce the utmost panic in the government, depriving it of its will to action by removing the cleverest and most energetic supporters.*

17. *The second group comprises those who will be spared for the time being in order that, by a series of monstrous acts, they may drive the people into inevitable revolt.*

18. *The third category consists of a great many brutes in high positions, distinguished neither by their cleverness nor thei energy, while enjoying riches, influence, power, and high positions by virute of their rank. These must be exploited in every possible way; they must be implicated and embroiled in our affairs, their dirty secrets must be ferreted out, and they must be transformed into slaves. Their power, influence, and connections, their wealth and their energy, will form an inexhaustable treasure and a precious help in all our undertakings.*

19. *The fourth category comprises ambitious office-holders and liberals of various shades of opinion. The revolutionary must pretend to collaborate with them, blindly following them, while at the same time, prying out their secrets until they are completely in his power. They must be so compromised that there is no way out for them, and then they can be used to create disorder in the State.*

20.   *The fifth category consists of those doctrinaires, conspirators, and revolutionists who cut a great figure on paper or in their cliques.   They must be constantly driven on to make compromising declarations: as a result, the majority of them will be destroyed, while a minority will become genuine revolutionaries.*

21.   **The sixth category is especially important: women.** *They can be divided into three main groups.   First, those frivilous, thoughtless, and vapid women, whom we shall use as we use the third and fourth category of men.   Second, women who are ardent, capable, and devoted, but whom do not belong to us because they have not yet achieved a passionless and austere revolutionary understanding; these must be used like the men of the fifth category.   Finally, there are the women who are completely on our side -- i.e., those who are wholly dedicated and who have accepted our program in its entirety.   We should regard these women as the most valuable or our treasures; without their help, we would never succeed.*

The Attitude of the Society toward the People

22.   *The Society has no aim other than the complete liberation and happiness of the masses -- i.e., of the people who live by manual labor.*   **Convinced that their emancipation and the achievement of this happiness can only come about as a result of an all-destroying popular revolt, the Society will use all its resources and energy toward increasing and intensfying the evils and miseries of the people until at last their patience is exhausted and they are   driven to a general uprising.**

23.   *By a revolution, the Society does not mean an orderly revolt according to the classic western model -- a revolt which always stops short of attacking the rights of property and the traditional social systems of so-called civilization and morality.   Until now, such a revolution has always limited itself to the overthrow of one political form in order to replace it by another, thereby attempting to bring about a so-called revolutionary state.*   **The only form of revolution beneficial to the people is one which destroys the entire State to the roots and exterminated all the state traditions, institutions, and classes** *in Russia.*

24.   *With this end in view, the Society therefore refuses to*

impose any new organization from above. Any future organization will doubtless work its way through the movement and life of the people; but this is a matter for future generations to decide. **Our task is terrible, total, universal, and merciless destruction.**

25. Therefore, in drawing closer to the people, we must above all make common cause with those elements of the masses which, since the foundation of the state of Muscovy, have never ceased to protest, not only in words but in deeds, against everything directly or indirectly connected with the state: against the nobility, the bureaucracy, the clergy, the traders, and the parasitic kulaks. **We must unite with the adventurous tribes of brigands, who are the only genuine revolutionaries in Russia.**

26. **To weld the people into one single unconquerable and all-destructive force -- this is our aim, our conspiracy, and our task.**

Here's a "catechism" ...

Of course, not all ordinary revolutionaries and not even all of their leaders in Russia of XIX-XX centuries were quite consistent with this "ideal", but in the biographies of each of the leaders of the Bolshevik seen this devilish fire of Nechayev's "catechism."

As for today's terrorists, who fight against the western civilization, as can be seen, "Catechism of a Revolutionary" is fully consistent with the ideology and methods of their struggle. Many of the provisions and recommendations of the "Catechism" literally fit their methods of struggle. We do not know, whether the ideologists and leaders of modern terrorists read this "Catechism", but it is so.

Lenin and Nechayev

Lenin not only appreciated Nechayev and considered him "titanium of revolution", but took a lot from him in matters of tactics and methods of combating opponents. In the first years after the October Revolution of 1917, Lenin even tried to build in Russia so-called "war communism" - by prescription of Nechayev.

Barracks communism (also referred to as Nechayevshchina)

is the term coined by Karl Marx to refer to a "crude," authoritarian, forced collectivism and communism, where all aspects of life are bureaucratically regimented and communal. In particular, Marx used the expression to criticise the vision of Sergey Nechayev, outlined in Fundamentals of the Future Social System.

Vladimir Lenin

The Lenin's attempt of "Barracks communism" in Russia (in 1917-1920) failed, but all the rest of his life (till his dead in 1924) Lenin very much appreciated the theory and practice of Sergei Nechayev.

In 1926 in Moscow the book by Bolshevik historian Alexander Gambarova "In disputes about Nechayev" [4] was published . In it he writes: "... *Nechayev went to the triumph of the social revolution by true means, and that in due his time he failed, the same after many years the Bolsheviks make, - Bolsheviks who were able to realize a lot of the tactical methods, first put forward by Nechayev.*"

According Gambarov, Nechayev was ahead of his time, and he was not only a Bolshevik, but Leninist. Having established what is Nechaevsky "Leninism" Qambarov writes: "*The revolution sanctifies all the means in the political struggle. For this basic maxim on Nechayev attacked all his political enemies and opponents (of Katkov to populists) and a whole galaxy of bourgeois historians, counting the "disgusting" inherent Nechayev "Machiavellianism." Anticipating this, Nechayev has repeatedly declared his "contempt for public opinion" and even proud of similar attacks against him. Hence the position that served Nechayev motto: "**Who is not with us is against us.**" Is not this the same motto guided mass in October 1917, when they went against the strongholds of capital against* *yesterday's false friends of the revolution? ".*

Let me correct Bolshevik historian: not mass, of course, but the Bolshevik leaders and their militias. In October 1917, there were still quite a bit. Anyway, but Gambarov found all the main characteristics of the Bolshevik communism in he Nechayev's ideology.

"Morality in politics is not. There is only expediency."

In the circle of his closest associates, Lenin admired Nechayev, calling it a "titanium revolution." When creating his own party and later Lenin always applied methods Nechayev and preached his ideas. And only in this light, mysterious ways and methods of the Bolshevik Party and the revolution became clear.

Vladimir Bonch-Bruevich, one of the closest associates of Lenin (from the founding days of the Bolshevik Party), wrote after the leader's death (in 1934) in the journal "Thirty Days" [5]:

<<*Till now Nechayev has not been studied by us. Vladimir Ilyich often wondered over Nechayev's leaflets - Lenin did it at the time when and while the word "Nechaev" and "Nechayevshina" even among his friends were almost swear words, when these terms would impose those who sought to propaganda of takeover proletariat to an armed uprising and unfailing pursuit of dictatorship of the proletariat, when Nechayev was called, as if it is particularly bad, "Russian Blancists" - Vladimir Ilyich often said what a neat trick done with Nechayev reactionaries with a light hand of Dostoevsky and his disgusting, but the genius of the novel "The Possessed", when even the revolutionary environment has negatively relate to Nechayev ... Vladimir Ilyich said:*

It is forgotten that Nechayev had a flair for the organizer, the ability to establish specific skills throughout secret work, was able to clothe their thoughts in such great statements that were memorable for a lifetime. Suffice it to recall his answer in one leaflet, when on the question "who should be destroy of the reigning house?" Nechayev gives an accurate answer:" all great litany "[2] After all, it is formulated so simple and clear that it is clear for everyone who lived at that time in Russia, when Orthodoxy prevailed when the vast majority anyway, for one reason or another, all pepole were in church, and everyone knew that royal house of Romanov is glorify up in the great litanies. **Who of the House of Romanov must be destroyed? – ask himself the easiest reader. Yes, the whole house of Romanovs! – He must give an answer himself. After all, it's just to genius."**

So repeatedly said Vladimir Ilyich.>>

We note in passing that these confessions of closest ally of Lenin are actually guilty verdict to him in the murder of Imperial family and their closest relatives (grand dukes and duchesses) in 1918. ...

In a speech given October 4, 1920 in Moscow, Lenin said [5]:

"Any morality out off class-straggle concepts we deny. We say that it is cheating. We say: morally is what serves to destroy the old exploiting society."

Before the dispersal of the Constituent Assembly (in January 1918) Lenin had a conversation with a group of Left Srs; as recalled S. Mstislavsky in his "Notes on Lenin", <<*Maria Spiridonova said very excitedly: said something about "hooliganism" and about a morality . Lenin immediately raised his eyebrows:*

"A morality is absent in politicst. There is only

expediency.>>[6, v. 5, c.166]**.**

In fact, Lenin considered as his main ally not so much "class-conscious proletariat" as – like Nechayev – human despair and brutality. Inciting daring members of its Central Committee, who did not believe in the success of the uprising, on the eve of the October Revolution (October 25, 1917), he wrote to them: *"On July 3-4, the uprising was a mistake ... there was no such" brutality "... Now the picture quite different ... Our victory is assured, because people already close to despair. "* [7, 34, p. 244].

---

2 Ekteniya (also Litany, Greek. - "Distribution, Continuous prayer"), in worship
   - title sequence prayer petitions. Litany - one of the main components of the
   worship, important part of the greater part of worship in the Orthodox Church.

So, to sum all of the above, we can make the following brief conclusion:

At the beginning of XX century and earlier, Russian society was confident that the policy (and external and internal) must be moral. And till 1917, Lenin could admire Nechayev only in a narrow range closest associates.

After the Bolshevik Revolution in 1917, many aspects of the theory and methods of Nechayev used most deeply in three directions. First, this "militant atheism" - a bitter struggle against religion and the Church, persecution and repression against the priests, and it was aggressive atheist propaganda too. Second, is the organization and work of the new "secret police" (Cheka-GPU-NKVD-KGB). Third, is the organization and work of the Comintern[3] - the organization whose task was to "incitement of the world revolution." Agents of the Comintern worked extensively around the world until the Second World War. Of course, the Bolshevik ideology was also imbued with the spirit of "Nechaevshchina" and often used some of his methods of organization and propaganda.

Although after 1991 the ideas of communism collapsed and greatly weakened in the new Russia (during the reign of Boris Yeltsin), nevertheless, "birthmarks" Bolshevik ideology (and "birthmarks" of Stalinism) is still going strong in some parts of the ruling elites in Kremlin. This remains a problem for the Russian civil society.

As for today's terrorists, who fight against the western civilization, as can be seen, "Catechism of a Revolutionary" is fully consistent with the ideology and methods of their struggle. Many of the provisions and recommendations of the "Catechism" literally fit their methods of struggle. We do not know, whether the ideologists and leaders of modern terrorists read this "Catechism", but it is so.

---

3   The Communist International, abbreviated as Comintern and also known as the Third International (1919–1943), was an international communist organization initiated in Moscow during March 1919. The International intended to fight "by all available means, including armed force, for the overthrow of the international bourgeoisie and for the creation of an international Soviet republic as a transition stage to the complete abolition of the State."

Literature

1. Heller, Mikhail (1988). Cogs in the Wheel. New York: Knopf. p. 12. ISBN 0-394-56926-1. "The Catechism of a Revolutionary, a chilling blueprint for the ideal "New Man," was the manifesto of a secret society called The People's Revenge (Narodnaya Rasprava).

2. Crenshaw, Martha (1995). Terrorism in Context. University Park: Pennsylvania State University Press. p. 72. ISBN 0-271-01015-0.

3. *Нечаев С. Г.,* Катехизис революционера / Революционный радикализм в России: век девятнадцатый. М.: Археографический центр, 1997. (С. 244-248).

4. *Гамбаров А. В.,* В спорах о Нечаеве. М.: Московский рабочий, 1926.

5. *Шуб Д. Н.,* Политические деятели России (1850-х—1920-х гг.) (гл. 2 "Русские предтечи Ленина" IV. Бакунин, Нечаев и Ленин). Нью-Йорк: Издание «Нового журнала», 1969.

6. Воспоминания о Владимире Ильиче Ленине. М.: Политиздат, 1990.

7. *Ленин В. И.,* Полное собрание сочинений, 5-е издание. М.: Издательство политической литературы, 1967.

8. Lucia de Jesus, Fátima In Lucia's Own Words (1995), The Ravengate Press, pp. 104

9. Папа Римский скрывает правду о будущем России. Лиза Сайфер. – Утро.ру, 11 ноября 2008

Era of a separation.

(Metaphysics of Good and Evil)

The vast majority of people (at least in Western civilization) perceives terrorism as an absolute evil - while the ideologues of modern terrorism consider an absolute evil just the Western civilization.

What is a Good and what is an Evil?

Starting these notes, I would been wanted immediately "take the bull by the horns" and to write about the moral (and immoral) aspects of the struggle between Good and Evil (satan and demons against God), but I soon realized that this subject can not do without a large preface about the metaphysics of the problem of Good and Evil in history humanity, without the story about the started in 2007 \ 2008 "Era of separation" between Good and Evil.

Preface. Four age (eras) of the Universe.

According to the cosmological ideas of ancient Zoroastrians, the existence of our Universe goes through four developmental cycle. Four age of the Universe - era of a creation, era of a mixing, era of a separation and era of a reunification. But these four eras are the eras not only of the Universe as a whole, but also the eras of the history of mankind. On Earth, in human history, each era of the Universe manifests itself in three worlds: in the world of ideas (the spiritual world), in the world of incarnation (the material world) and in the interim between these two world (world of soul). These three worlds are that in what we are really manifesting: spirit, soul and body - or, thought, word and deed.

That is, each of the four eras realizes its tendencies in three forms (mentioned above), total - twelve vectors of development. Zoroastrian doctrine (or rather, "zeroanism", by name of main zoroastrian god Zeroana - the god of time) symbolically connects all this also with astrology, with signs of the Zodiac. In this context, the four quadrants of the Zodiac symbolically represent the four eras of human development, and the three signs of the Zodiac in each quadrant is symbolically linked to the three worlds.

The duration of each of the four eras is different. At the beginning of the creation of the Universe (and at the beginning of human history), a time was as if stretched, the time went as if slowly, but by the end of the world cycle (and by the end of human history) time will be compressed, will be accelerated (and it already take place) - so the length of each time period (era) is different in different periods of the existence of the Universe.

We can assume that the last stage (recently ended) of the era of mixing coincided with the age (era) known in esoteric as the age (era) of Pisces. This age lasted about 2,160 years (the so-called "cosmic month" 1 \ 12 of the precession cycle of the axis of the Earth - the "cosmic year"). Beginning in 2007 \ 2008, the age (era) of Aquarius will also continue for 2,160 years ("cosmic month"), but, **I believe, the era of separation (which began in 2007 \ 2008) will last about 165 years (Neptune cycle). I believe that this era is also a time of the Apocalypse** (St. John the Theologian) - more information can be found in my brochure "Timeline of the Apocalypse of John's Revelation" (in English):

https://www.amazon.com/Timeline-Apocalypse-Johns-Revelation-2008-ebook/dp/B00I77XG7C/ref=la_B009HTVPLS_1_11?s=books&ie=UTF8&qid=1469798313&sr=1-11#nav-subnav

or (in Russian) in my article "Apocalypse 2008-2173» (http://www.proza.ru/2008/06/05/45)

Before moving on to practical reasoning, we must still briefly describe the essence of each of the four eras. I quote below (abridged) on the text of the "Four era of the Universe» (http://www.zoroastrian.ru/node/1220), from the book "The teachings of the ancient Aryans" (M.2007) by Pavel Globa, with my comments and additions :

Era of Creation

This era includes three stages, which symbolically correspond to the first three signs of the Zodiac: Aries - the initial impetus and the emergence of Zeroana's design of the creation of our World, Taurus - the material realization of Zeroana's design (the implementation of our World), Gemini - the establishment of internal relations and laws of existence and development of our World. During this period, the Lord (Ahura-Mazda \Ohrmazd\ in Zoroastrianism) creates all creations (parts and particles), at first in the ideal world (world of ideas), then gives to every particle a self-consciousness, and later - and the material body. It was a perfect world, inside which any evil could not occur . It was only towards the end of the third stage of this era, when the World gets materialization when every particle of the world understands that it itself is not just a piece of something a whole, but also something in itself contains a substance that is able to make decisions and do a choice - that's only at that time an Evil start to occur. That is, until the end of the first era (symbolically in Gemini) devil appears. Devil - Angra Manyu \ Ahriman in Zoroastrianism. Figuratively speaking, the evil (Ahriman) is an entity wich realized itself before other entities, and has made a choice in favor of evil - that is, against the Creator (against Ohrmazd). But while this is not an invasion of evil into the world. This is the place and time of the first collision Ohrmazd and Ahriman, light and darkness, Good and Evil, as well as the free primary choice. According to Zoroastrian concept, it was the time of some "agreement" between Ohrmazd (god) and Ahriman (devil) about the rules of struggle for souls of people . Spirit of Light (Spenta Manyu in Zoroastrianism) realizes himself and choses an eternity, and the spirit of darkness (Ahriman \ Angra Manyu in Zoroastrianism) realizes himself and choses a temporary (world of material transient values). Here is main mystery of myth of Gemini. Our World at that time has reached the lowest point of the Zodiac (1st degree of Cancer sign).

In the Christian tradition this time corresponds to those time of the Old Testament, when Lucifer was not yet fallen angel and "walked with God", and had to ask His permission to test a faith of righteous Job ...

Era of Mixing

Then comes the era of mixing, and at this transitional moment the spirit of Darkness (Angra Manyu \ Ahriman) invades into our World. This era determines the period of time associated with a mixing of Good and evil. Zodiac symbolically linked with this era through the signs of Cancer, Leo and Virgo. The sign of Cancer symbolically associated with the emergence of life on Earth (life originated in water). This sign is associated with the original gene pool of humanity, with a race, roots, past (water - custodian of information). It was at this time Fravashi (the souls of the first ancestors of all people) have given their consent to descend to Earth to incarnate (in body) for a fight against evil. The sign of Leo (Leo's period) corresponds to the age of ancient kingdoms and the Old Testament. The sign of Virgo is associated with a ruling law of era of mixing, and this ruling law is concerned with the choice between Good and evil. The sign of Virgo - the world of Soul of the second quadrant of the Zodiac (era of mixing), that is the soul of human facing the choice: either the soul must remain pure, or soul should mix a Good and evil (Light and darkness). Choosing the side of darkness - is slavery and subjection. Choosing the side of Light - noble service and duty.

This last stage of the era of mixing coincided with the zodiacal era of Pisces, which began about 150 BC The era of Pisces is associated with Christianity. The very beginning of the era of Pisces is associated with the precursors of Christianity: with the Essenes and their Teacher of Righteousness, who was crucified on the cross about 150 BC [Igor Tantlevsky. Introduction to the Pentateuch. M., 2000]. See also my book "Astro-Biblos', published in 1995, or online - my article "Apocalypse 2008-2173»: http://www.proza.ru/2008/06/ 05/45 .

As I mentioned earlier, in the times of Old Testament, Satan has communed with God in heaven, "walked with God", and God allowed him to test the faith of Job (according the Book of Job). Since the days of the New Testament, when, according to the testimony of Jesus Christ, Satan was cast out of heaven ("I saw Satan fall from heaven like lightning" [Luke 10, 18].) - From now on, according to the Apostle Paul [2 Cor. 12, 7-9], what accord has Christ with Belial? - That is, with the evangelical times between God and Satan there can not be any agreements, in contrast to the times of Job (the Old Testament).

In fact, this main distinction relationships of God and Devil in the Old Testament and the New Testament is extremely important not only for every believer, but also for

understanding of world history.

So, the last part of era of mixing began about 150 BC and continued until recently, to 2007 \ 2008.

Era of Separation

So, finally, after such a long preface, we come to the present time. So, in 2007 \ 2008 began the process of transition to the next era. This era of separation - the period of time associated with the division between Good and evil in our world. Symbolically in the circle of Zodiac, our time complies with transition from the lower to the upper hemisphere of Zodiac, and this transition occurs through destructive (1st) degree of the sign of Libra - the collective degree of humanity. The answer to the question "whom do you serve?" Is realizing and manifesting here. That is, during this period there is started an ideological division between Good and evil (the realization of the world of ideas, in Libra).

According to my estimates, humanity will be held this destructive 1st degree of Libra no more than 16-18 years. That is, the separated position of Good and evil in our world will be determined not later 2025. However, maybe, these positions are largely already decided in 2014-2016. Subsequently, I hope to write more about this period, but now we will continue an overview of the era of separation.

As I noted earlier, the era of separation (as a whole) will continue for about 165 years (until about 2173), but I do not know yet how many years will continue the ages of the signs of Libra, Scorpio and Sagittarius separately. Passage of mankind through the sign of Scorpio will be followed by the most serious tests in the embodied world - those trials and disasters that are described in Revelation.

Ophiuchus's age (the last 7 degrees of Scorpio and the first 7 degrees of Sagittarius), respectively, will bring the most terrible trials and complete purification and liberation.

The last period of the era of division corresponds to the sign of Sagittarius - the division between good and evil at the level of every human soul, followed by a separation of time and space. It is the transition from Sagittarius into Capricorn there will final separation of light and darkness in our world and in the heart of every person.

Thus, in 2008-2025, we are at the beginning of the Era of Separation, when it is not so simple (as it sometimes seems) to make a choice between Good and evil. But just in these years, many make this choice.

Era of Recreating

This last era is symbolically manifested through the zodiacal signs of Capricorn, Aquarius and Pisces. Here there will be a recreating (liberation and complete purification) of Spirit, Body and Soul. It is a victory over the devil (Angra Manyu in Zoroastrian tradition), deprivation of its original identity, the liberation of the Incarnate World and the union of all souls in a single living organism. In this last era there will be complete disembodiment of Evil. It will lose its strength: Saturn (the ruler of Capricorn) will complete the compression of evil at the level of ideas in the sign of Capricorn. That's why Capricorn is the highest point of the Zodiac: this sign is associated with the final victory over evil.

Cleansing the body (cleansing of the material world) is associated with the sign of Aquarius, with the mystery of dead and living water: dead water connects the disparate (separated one off others) parts of the body, the living water gives them alive spirit. Each person's body becomes divine; the earthly World will be transformed as a reflection of the upper World. And finally, the fusion of souls in a single image of the World Soul will happen in the sign of Pisces ...

Prior to the era of recreating there is still very, very far away. I believe that it will start after the time of the Apocalypse (according the book of Revelation of John). This era described there by the words "will be a new heaven and a new earth." As I mentioned earlier, in my estimation, the time of the Apocalypse - is the 2008-2173 years. See my brochure "Timeline of the Apocalypse of John's Revelation" (in English):

https://www.amazon.com/Timeline-Apocalypse-Johns-Revelation-2008-ebook/dp/B00I77XG7C/ref=la_B009HTVPLS_1_11?s=books&ie=UTF8&qid=1469798313&sr=1-11#nav-subnav

or (in Russian) in my article "Apocalypse 2008-2173» (http://www.proza.ru/2008/06/05/45).

Our time: the beginning of the era of separation.

Thus, some modern esoterics believe that the era of separation began in 2007 \ 2008 (and I support this view). Now, in 2016, the sacral mystery of the transition from the era of mixing to the era of separation of Good and Evil became apparent (at least for many people). Of course, we need to understand that evil is not identified itself with evil neither earlier nor now. Evil feels itself rightly, but after the 2007\2008 (or even earlier, after September 11, 2001), people of good will see evil much more clearly than 10-15 years ago. And the confrontation between Good and Evil is now really much more openly and obviously to many people - both in politics and in public morality. But not all people are beginning to see clearly.

Where Good and where evil where? - As you can see, this issue is likely to remain open. Since we are still at the very beginning of the Era of Separation, and it (the separation of the forces of Good and Evil) only started in recent years.

www.ingramcontent.com/pod-product-compliance
Lightning Source LLC
Chambersburg PA
CBHW060446290526
45793CB00002B/594